homemade gifts
with love

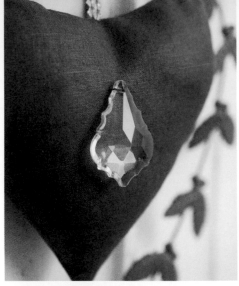

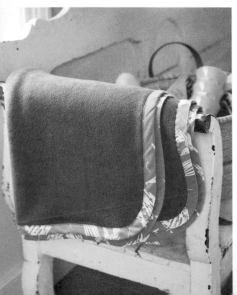

homemade gifts
with love

over **35** beautiful handcrafted gifts
to make and give

catherine woram

CICO BOOKS
LONDON NEW YORK

Published in 2010 by CICO Books
An imprint of Ryland Peters & Small
20–21 Jockey's Fields   519 Broadway, 5th Floor
London WC1R 4BW   New York, NY 10012

10 9 8 7 6 5 4 3 2 1

A CIP catalog record for this book is available from
the Library of Congress and the British Library.

ISBN-13: 978-1-907030-71-0

Printed in China

Designer: Jacqui Caulton
Photographer: Emma Mitchell
(pages 56–57, 60–65, and 98–101 by Carolyn Barber)

contents

Introduction 6

chapter 1:
seasonal celebrations

Valentine cookies 10
Easter flowers bowl 12
Felt egg cozies 14
Painted eggs 16
Christmas stocking 18
Clove pomander 22
Candied orange peel 24

chapter 2:
special occasions

Flower corsage 28
Chandelier drop heart 30
Father's day apron 34
Decoupage frame 36
Monogrammed pillows 38
Picnic basket & rug 42
Beaded photo album 46

chapter 3:
for the girls

Lavender hearts 52
Friendship bracelet 54
Ring of roses basket 56
Candle votives 58
Gardener's gift 60
Spring bulb planter 64
Evening bag 66

chapter 4:
at home

New home card 72
Fabric bunting 74
Wax candle cups 76
Patchwork teapot cozy 78
Stenciled wooden tray 82
Decoupage coasters 84
Embroidered pillow 86
Beaded throw 88

chapter 5:
babies & children

Appliqué blanket 94
Baby basket 98
Baby towel & facecloth set 102
Painted alphabet 106
Stenciled child's chair 108
Russian dolls 110
Pompom book bag 112
Felt cellphone case 114

Templates 116
Useful addresses 127
Index 128

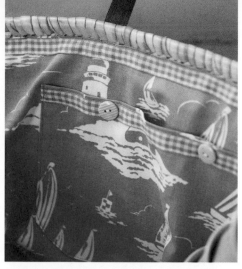

introduction

A handmade gift is truly special and shows that you have spent time, effort, and love in its creation. When you make a gift yourself it can also be personalized or customized, so you can always give the perfect present. In this book you will find more than 35 great ideas for handmade gifts that are suitable for christenings, weddings, and engagements, as well as seasonal presents for Christmas, Easter, and Valentine's Day, and delightful gifts for newborn babies and children. Create a welcoming card to give to a new neighbor, or cut up old map prints to make simple but stylish coasters and a matching picture frame.

The projects in this book cover a wide range of crafts, from sewing projects featuring embroidery, patchwork, or beading, to others based on painting, stenciling, decoupage, or baking. Each project is accompanied by simple step-by-step photographs, as well as useful tips to help you achieve great results. You will also find all the templates you need at the back of the book.

The easier projects—such as the pretty wool pompoms and decoupage frames—can be made by children, who will love the crafting elements involved and truly enjoy creating their own personal gifts for friends and family. All the projects are very easy to follow and I hope they will help you to create your own homemade gifts made with love. And, as the perfect finishing touch, at the very end of the book, there is a sheet of stick-on gift labels to use when wrapping your creation.

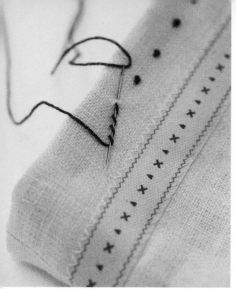

chapter 1

seasonal celebrations

From delicious heart-shaped cookies for Valentine's Day to beautifully detailed heirloom stockings for Christmas, this chapter will give you plenty of ideas for seasonal gifts using fabrics, paint, and paper. Recycle old newsprint to create the shapely decoupage bowl decorated with delicate paper flowers, use brightly colored felt to create fun egg cozies for a perfect Easter breakfast, or make traditional pomanders from cloves and oranges and finished with red grosgrain ribbon.

valentine cookies

Make these delicious heart-shaped cookies and decorate them with colorful frosting and a pretty bow. Wrap them in a cellophane bag tied with matching ribbon as a gift for Valentine's Day.

you will need

6 tbsp unsalted butter

½ cup (100g/3½oz) superfine (caster) sugar

1 large egg

1½ cups (150g/5¼oz) all-purpose (plain) flour

½ tsp baking powder

½ tsp salt

Tubes of ready-mixed frosting and frosting flowers

Ribbon

Cellophane bags

Sharp scissors

1 Cream the butter and sugar together in a bowl until soft, then beat the egg into the mixture. Sieve in the flour, baking powder, and salt. Roll the dough into a ball, wrap in plastic, and chill in the refrigerator for about an hour. Sprinkle some flour onto a flat surface, then roll the dough to a thickness of about ¼in. (6mm). Cut out heart shapes using a cookie cutter—this quantity should make about 25 hearts.

2 Use a drinking straw to pierce a hole at the center top of each heart cookie prior to baking. Grease a flat baking sheet and space the cookies evenly across the sheet. Bake the cookies for 10–12 minutes at 350ºF (180ºC/Gas mark 4)—the thinner the cookie is rolled, the shorter the cooking time.

3 When the heart cookies are golden brown, remove the baking sheet from the oven and transfer the cookies to a wire tray until they are completely cool. Use tubes of white and red ready-mixed frosting to apply tiny dots around the edge of each cookie.

4 Use a dab of frosting to stick a frosting flower to the center of each heart and let dry. Cut an 8in. (20cm) length of ribbon for each cookie and thread through the pierced hole. Tie the ribbon in a bow, then trim the ribbon ends across diagonally with sharp scissors to prevent them from fraying.

tip

Make these cookies using an egg-shaped cutter for Easter, and use lengths of ribbon to hang them from white painted twigs as an edible decoration.

easter flowers bowl

This delicate bowl is made from layers of papier mâché and makes a great gift for any occasion—this one is filled with foil-wrapped Easter eggs. Pretty paper flowers and miniature buttons are used to decorate the bowl so it's a great project for children.

you will need

Bowl or plate to use as a mold

Plastic food wrap

Newsprint

White PVA glue

Thick brush for glue

White undercoat

Green paint

Paintbrushes

Hot glue gun

Paper flowers

Small buttons

1 Place the bowl mold upside down on a flat surface and cover the outside with a layer of plastic wrap, folding the edges under to the inside. Tear all the newsprint roughly into strips approx. 1 x 2in. (2.5 x 5cm).

2 Lay two or three strips of newsprint on the bowl mold and apply a layer of glue. Continue pasting strips until the mold is completely covered. You will need about 8–10 layers of paper to create a sturdy bowl.

3 Leave the papier mâché on its mold to dry in a warm, dry place—do not place on a heater or anywhere too hot, as this can cause cracking. The bowl will take at least a day to dry completely. When the papier mâché is dry, carefully ease it off the mold and peel off the plastic wrap.

4 Paint the papier mâché bowl with a base coat of white undercoat and allow to dry. Then paint the bowl with the green paint and allow to dry thoroughly. Apply a further coat of paint for complete coverage, if required. Use the hot glue gun to stick the paper flowers around the inside rim of the bowl. Finish with a small button in the center of each flower.

tip

Try using colored tissue paper to create a delicate bowl— the tissue paper hardens with the PVA glue but retains a very pretty, slightly translucent finish.

felt egg cozies

A great Easter gift, these colorful cozies feature bunny ears and are made in bright felt decorated with simple contrast stitching and fun felt flowers.

you will need

Paper and pencil for copying template

Scissors

Pins

10in. (25cm) square felt per egg cozy

Contrasting embroidery floss

Sewing needle

Felt flowers to decorate

3-D fabric paint

Fabric glue

1 Copy the egg cozy template on page 119 onto paper and cut out. Pin the pattern to the felt and cut out two pieces of felt for each egg cozy. Pin the two pieces of felt together and blanket-stitch on one side from the bottom (scalloped) edge of the egg cozy to the base of the ears.

2 When you reach the ears, continue in blanket stitch around the ear, working on only one layer of felt so that the two ears are separate. Repeat around the other ear and then continue in blanket stitch down the other side of the egg cozy through both layers of felt.

3 Using the 3-D fabric paint, make a small dot in the center of each scallop along the bottom of the egg cozy on one side and let dry—this can take about an hour. When dry, repeat on the other side of the egg cozy.

4 Use fabric glue to stick three felt flowers to each side of the egg cozy. Allow the glue to dry completely.

tip

These would make a great Easter gift combined with an egg cup and chocolate egg and presented in a cellophane bag tied with a pretty ribbon.

painted eggs

Graphic letters cut from newsprint and magazines are used to decorate these simple painted eggs. Display in a papier-mâché bowl decorated with similar letters.

you will need

Blown eggs or plastic eggs for painting

White undercoat

Paintbrushes

Selection of colored paints

Spoon for holding egg

Selection of newsprint pages

Scissors

Glue

Water-based acrylic varnish (optional)

1 If you are using fresh eggs, pierce them top and bottom with a sharp pin and blow through the hole to remove the yolk and albumen. Wash the eggs carefully. Give each egg a layer of undercoat and leave to dry completely.

2 Paint the eggs in different colors using a medium paintbrush and let dry completely. Apply a further coat of paint for complete coverage, if required. You may find it easier to rest the egg in a spoon while painting to prevent it rolling around.

3 Cut out letters in different colors and sizes from newsprint using scissors. Make sure the letters are no bigger than about 1in. (2.5cm) square or they will not fit smoothly over the curved shell of the egg and will crease when stuck on.

4 Glue one letter to each egg using a fine layer of glue applied with a paintbrush. Once all the letters are in place, if you wish you can apply a coat of water-based acrylic varnish over each egg to protect the paint and paper letters and make them more durable.

tip

Display the eggs in a papier-mâché bowl made following the instructions on page 12. Decorate the sides of the bowl to match the eggs with an assortment of letters cut from newsprint.

christmas stocking

This country-style Christmas stocking decorated with pretty buttons and embroidery is guaranteed to become a family heirloom! It would make a perfect Christmas gift—personalize it with initials or dates to make it even more special.

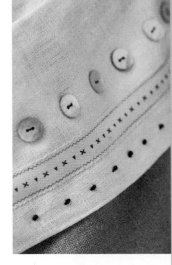

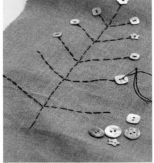
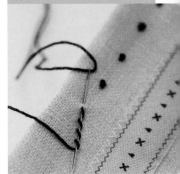

1 Copy the stocking template on page 126 and the stocking cuff template on page 117 onto paper, and cut both out. Fold the pieces of fabric in half and pin on the two templates. Cut out two stocking shapes in the oatmeal linen and two cuff pieces in the cream linen.

2 Copy the Christmas tree shape on page 117 onto one piece of the stocking section using a fabric pencil. Begin working the embroidery in a simple running stitch, using three strands of six-strand embroidery thread. Keep stitching until you have filled in the tree shape and all the branches.

3 Use embroidery floss to sew a pearl button to the top and bottom of the tree, and at the end of each branch. Work two or three stitches through each button to make sure they are secure. With right sides facing, stitch the two cuff pieces together at both side seams. Press seams flat and turn the cuff right side out.

4 Fold the top and bottom edges of the cuff inside by 1in. (2.5cm) and press. Topstitch the ribbon along the bottom edge of the cuff through both layers of fabric approx. 1in. (2.5cm) from the bottom. Use embroidery floss to work small French knots along the bottom edge of the cuff, approx. ½in. (12mm) apart and through both layers of fabric.

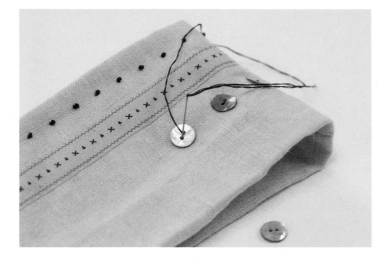

5 Stitch the remaining pearl buttons along the top edge of the cuff approx. 2in. (5cm) from the fold using the embroidery floss, stitching through one layer of fabric only. Each button should be spaced approx. ⅞in. (2cm) apart.

6 With right sides facing, stitch the two stocking sections together around all edges, leaving the top (straight edge) open. Trim and notch the seam allowance on the curved sections. Turn the stocking to the right side and slide it inside the cuff, so that the cuff sits with the top edge of the stocking inside the folded top edge of the cuff.

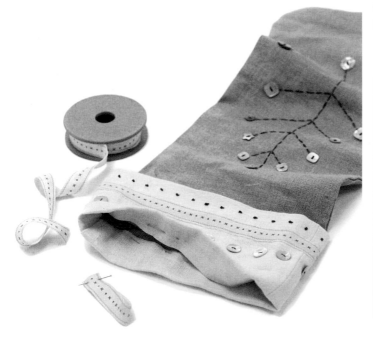

7 Pin the cuff to the top of the stocking, folding under the raw edge of the cuff inside the stocking as you work. Stitch the cuff to the inside of the stocking by hand using whipstitch and matching sewing thread.

8 Cut a length of ribbon approx. 2½in. (6.5cm) in length and fold in half, then fold the ends to the inside by ¼in. (6mm). Stitch the loop to the inside of the stocking on the outside edge using whipstitch.

variation

Make the stocking in bright colors—such as red and lime green with colorful plastic buttons—as the perfect Christmas gift for a child. You could also personalize the stocking by adding a name or initials in embroidery around the cuff.

clove
pomander

Pomanders made with oranges and decorated with cloves are a tradition at Christmas. With their sweet, spicy fragrance they make a lovely gift, or they can be used as pretty decorations to hang at home.

you will need

Pen

Large orange

Bradawl (for piercing orange)

Cloves

24in. (60cm) of ½in. (12mm) wide velvet ribbon

Scissors

Pins

Glue or hot glue gun

1 Use the pen to draw the position of the ribbon on the orange; it will be wrapped around the orange in the shape of a cross at right angles. Use the bradawl to pierce the holes for the cloves all over the orange within the four quarters between the ribbon lines.

2 You may find it easier to work one quarter of the orange at a time. Carefully push the sharp end of the clove into the orange. The top ends of the clove can be very brittle so push the cloves in gently to avoid breaking them off. Continue to push the cloves into the orange until all four quarters are fully covered.

tip

Pomanders also make great decorations for the Christmas tree—use different colored ribbons, such as green, red, and plum, to tie them on.

3 Wrap a length of ribbon around the orange and fix to the base by pushing a pin through the two ends and into the orange. Attach another piece of ribbon to the base and wrap around to the top of the orange, making a loop approx. 2in (5cm) high at the top. Insert a pin through the rIbbon to hold in place—you may like to put a dab of glue on the ribbon for added security.

4 Tie a bow in ribbon and glue to the base of the hanging loop using glue or the hot glue gun.

candied orange peel

These delicious chocolate-coated slivers of orange peel are very easy to make and look especially pretty when presented in a crisp white gift box. The combination of citrus and chocolate makes a perfect after-dinner treat.

you will need

4 large oranges

Chopping board and sharp knife

4¼ cups (1 litre/1¾ pints) water

1½ cups (275g/9¾oz) superfine (caster) sugar

Saucepan

Parchment paper

10oz (300g) good-quality dark (plain) chocolate

Bowl

1¾yd. (1.5m) gingham ribbon

Scissors

1 Cut the orange into quarters and remove as much of the pith as possible using a sharp knife, but without damaging the peel of the orange. Cut the peel into strips approx. ½in. (12mm) wide using the sharp knife. Set aside on the chopping board.

2 Place the water and sugar in the saucepan, bring to the boil, and boil for 5 minutes. Add the orange peel strips and simmer in the sugar and water mixture for about 2 hours—during this time the mixture should reduce significantly. Remove from the heat and allow to cool. Drain the peel and leave to cool on parchment paper.

3 Break the chocolate into small chunks and melt in a bowl over a saucepan of simmering water, stirring to help break the pieces down quickly. Dip the orange peel strips in the chocolate so that approx. half their length is covered. Place the strips back on the parchment paper and leave to cool completely.

4 Tie the chocolate-coated citrus sticks together in bundles of three with short lengths of gingham ribbon tied in a simple knot. Trim the ribbon ends diagonally to prevent them fraying.

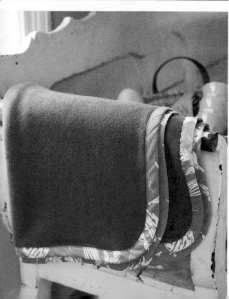

chapter 2
special occasions

This chapter contains a delightful selection of gift ideas to celebrate special occasions, such as Father's Day, Mother's Day, weddings, and engagements. The stunning beaded photo album would make the perfect wedding gift, while a pair of delicately embroidered heart pillows would be ideal for an anniversary or a betrothal present. Featuring wired beading, ribbon embroidery, decoupage, stenciling, and simple sewing, the projects in this chapter use a range of crafting techniques.

flower corsage

Give a gift to treasure on Mother's Day with this delicate corsage brooch, made from tiny rocaille beads and fine wire, and finished with a pearl bead center.

you will need

2 tubes/boxes rocaille beads in mauve and pink

22 gauge (0.6mm) beading wire

Pearl bead for center

Strong scissors for cutting wire

Small brooch back

Strong glue

1 Begin threading mauve rocaille beads onto wire to create the first petal shape. Bend the end of the wire backward so the beads do not fall off—leave approx. 6in. (15cm) of wire at the end to finish the brooch. Thread approx. 50 beads for a large petal, then twist the wire ends together to set the petal shape, and begin threading the next. When you have made the first set of petals, twist the ends of the wire together several times through the center of the flower to finish.

2 Make the smaller pink flower in the same way, using approx. 30 rocaille beads for each petal. Thread the wire ends through the center petal shapes several times to secure in place.

3 Lay the smaller flower on top of the larger one and use the wire to wrap around the center, twisting it as you go to secure the two flower shapes together.

4 Thread the pearl bead onto one wire end and pull the wire over the center of the flower and toward the back of the brooch to position the bead in the center of the brooch. Wrap and twist the ends of the wire to the underside of the bead and push to the back of the brooch. Twist the ends together and trim off using scissors. Fix the flower to the brooch back with strong glue.

tip

Wired flowers are very versatile and can be made in different sizes to decorate many items. Glue one to the corner of a picture frame or to a card for a special occasion. Sew a smaller version to a length of velvet ribbon to create a pretty bracelet.

chandelier drop heart

Any romantic will love this decorative fabric heart in charcoal gray linen, decorated with a glass droplet salvaged from a chandelier. Hang it up anywhere using the delicate beaded loop.

you will need

Paper and pencil for copying template

Scissors

8 x 16in. (20 x 40cm) piece of gray linen

Pins

Sewing thread to match the linen and needle

Sewing machine

Polyester fiberfill (stuffing)

Strong sewing thread

Clear beads

Chandelier droplet (or similar from a craft shop)

1 Copy the heart template on page 116 onto paper, and cut out with scissors. Use this as a pattern to cut two hearts from the gray linen. Pin the two fabric sections together, right sides facing, and baste (tack).

2 Use a sewing machine to stitch around the heart shapes, leaving an opening of approx. 1½in. (4cm) on one of the straight edges. Trim off the excess thread and remove the basting stitches.

3 Trim and notch the seam allowance on the curved edges of the heart and trim away excess fabric from the pointed corner at the bottom of the heart. Turn the heart right side out and press flat using a hot iron.

tip

Use an equal mix of polyester fiberfill and dried lavender flowers to create a fragrant heart to hang from a door handle or in a bedroom closet.

4 Push the fiberfill stuffing into the heart through the opening in the side, using the pointed ends of the scissors to push it into the corners. Fill the heart until it is well stuffed and firm.

5 Hand-stitch the side opening in the heart closed using a small whipstitch and matching sewing thread. You may find it easier to pin the opening closed before sewing.

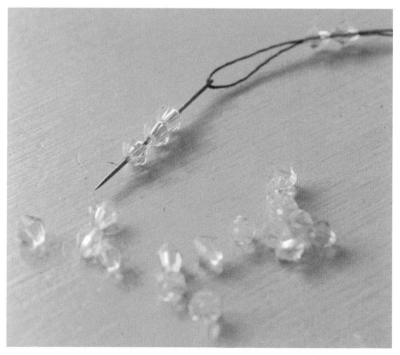

6 Slide the clear beads onto a needle threaded with strong sewing thread to form the hanging loop. Thread on enough beads to make a beaded length of approx. 7¼in. (18cm).

7 Using the beaded thread, take a stitch with the needle through the heart at the center dip point. Pull the beads tight, then thread the needle through the last bead to form the loop. Work several stitches to make sure that the loop is secure.

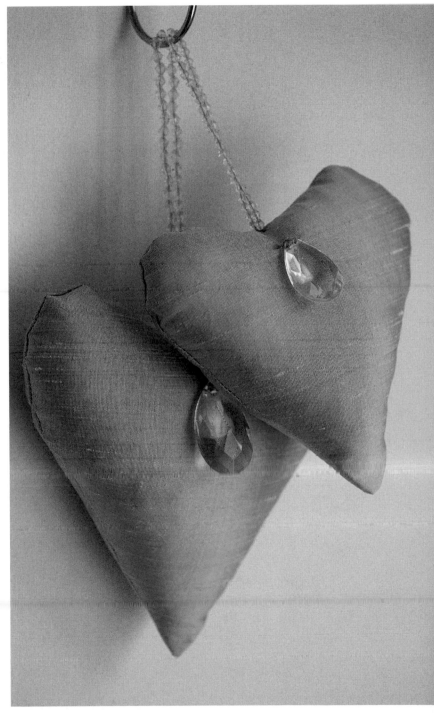

8 Use strong thread to stitch the chandelier droplet to the front of the padded heart to finish.

father's day apron

For a dad who loves to cook or barbecue, this stenciled apron, with its bold design of radishes, cabbages, and beans, is the perfect gift.

you will need

Paper and pencil for copying templates

1¼yd. (1m) of 55in. (137cm) wide cotton fabric

Scissors and safety pin

Needle and thread

Sewing machine

Vegetable stencils and stencil brush

Fabric stencil paints

Paper towel

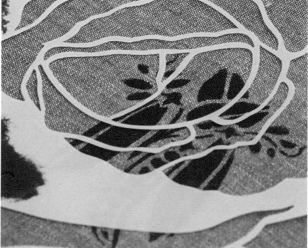

1 Copy the apron template on page 126 and the pocket shape on page 116 onto paper and cut out. Pin the patterns to the fabric and cut out. Also cut two waist ties and one neck strap, all measuring 2 x 30in. (5 x 75cm). Taking the main apron piece, fold a double ½in. (12mm) around all edges, pin in place, then machine-stitch. Fold the sides and bottom of the pocket section to the inside by ½in. (12mm) and baste (tack) in place. Machine stitch along these edges to hold the fold in place. Fold the top edge of the pocket section to the inside by 1in. (2.5cm), baste in place and then topstitch the fold. Press the main apron and the pocket section flat using a hot iron.

2 Position one of the stencils on the lower edge of the apron. Dip the stencil brush in the paint and use a piece of paper towel to blot off excess paint to prevent it bleeding beneath the stencil. Fill in the stencil motif with the paint by stippling the brush up and down over the stencil. Allow the paint to dry thoroughly. Repeat with different stencils to create a pattern along the bottom edge, and then stencil a design at the top of the apron.

tip

For a more feminine design, try using a stencil of pretty flowers or Shaker-style hearts. You could also use buttons to add 3-D detail to your design.

3 Stencil a different design on the pocket in the same way. Pin the pocket to the apron and baste in place along the sides and bottom edges. Topstitch in place using a sewing machine.

4 Fold a tie in half lengthwise, right sides facing, and press. Stitch the long edge then trim excess fabric from the seam. Pin a safety pin on one end and feed back through the tube of fabric to turn right side out. Repeat for the other tie and neck strap. Turn one end of each tie inside and stitch across. Stitch the other end of each tie to the sides of the apron. Stitch the neck strap to the top apron corners.

decoupage frame

Old maps used to decorate a simple picture frame make an unusual and eyecatching gift. See page 84 for matching coasters.

See page 84

you will need

- Copyright-free map images
- Pencil and ruler
- Scissors
- Plain wood picture frame
- White PVA glue
- Paintbrushes
- Water-based acrylic varnish

1 Use scissors to cut the map images into squares approx. ⅞ x ⅞in. (2 x 2cm) and rectangles approx. 1¼ x ⅞in. (3 x 2cm). Lay these out roughly over the picture frame to work out how many pieces of decoupage you will need.

2 Apply a fine layer of glue all over the back of the paper and glue the first piece of decoupage to one corner of the picture frame. You may find it easier to apply the glue with a paintbrush.

3 Once you have fixed the first piece in place, continue to glue pieces all over the rest of the frame. Overlap pieces slightly as you glue so that the entire picture frame is covered.

4 Once all the paper decoupage pieces are in place, leave the glue to dry completely. To finish, use a paintbrush to apply a thin layer of water-based acrylic varnish all over the frame.

tip

Also try using offcuts of wallpaper or leftover scraps of giftwrap for decoupage.

GULF OF MEXICO
MERIDA
MAYAPAN
IZAMAL
CHICHEN ITZA
UXMAL
KABAH
LABNA
YUCATAN
CHAKANPUTUN
BAKHALAL
CAMPECHE
TABASCO
PALENQUE
PIEDRAS NEGRAS
YAXCHILAN
TZENDALES
CHIAPAS
TIKAL
NARANJO
SEIBAL
BRITISH HONDURAS
QUEN SANTO
GUATEMALA
QUIRIGUA
HONDURAS
COPAN
SAN SALVADOR
PACIFIC OCEAN

monogrammed pillows

The perfect betrothal gift or wedding present, these heart-shaped pillows are stitched with silk ribbon, and decorated with felt flowers and the embroidered initials of the happy couple.

you will need

Paper and pencil for copying templates

16in. (40cm) of 55in. (137cm) wide cream linen fabric

Scissors or pinking shears

Fabric pencil

Embroidery floss and needle

Small felt flowers

Needle and thread

Small blue beads

Thin silk ribbon in assorted colors

Needle with wide eye for the ribbon

Sewing machine

Heart-shape pillow form or fiberfill (stuffing)

1 Copy the heart templates on pages 118 and 119 onto paper and cut out with scissors. Pin the patterns to the fabric and cut out a front and two back heart shapes. You may find it easier to cut out the fabric with pinking shears to help prevent the edges from fraying as you embroider. Use the fabric pencil to draw your chosen letter onto the fabric.

2 Begin working the initial on the front piece in chain stitch and three strands of six-strand embroidery floss in the color of your choice. When you have finished the embroidery, press the fabric flat on the reverse using a hot iron.

3 Hand-stitch the felt flowers onto the front, using the photograph opposite as a guide for their positioning. The heart pillow shown here has five flowers in total, but you could add more or fewer flowers if you prefer.

tip

You could make small square pillows instead of hearts and embroider the couple's full names or wedding date on the front instead of their initials.

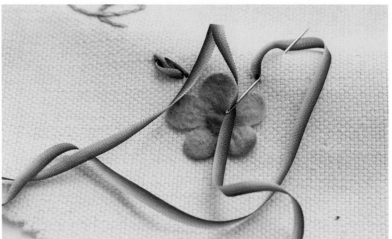

4 When you have finished sewing on the felt flowers, stitch a single bead to the center of each using the needle and thread. Secure the bead with several stitches and fasten off at the back of the fabric.

5 Carefully thread a length of silk ribbon into the large eye needle trying to keep it as flat as possible. Work a single chain stitch in silk ribbon between each felt flower petal—keep the ribbon as flat as you can while sewing. Work single chain stitches around the other flowers, as marked. Stitch the leaves in green ribbon in the positions shown in the photographs here.

6 With right sides facing, pin the two back sections of the pillow cover together. Use a sewing machine to stitch the center seam by approx. 2in. (5cm) up from the pointed end of the heart, then repeat at the top end, leaving the center of the seam open. Press the seam flat, making sure both sections are pressed to the same side.

7 With right sides facing, baste (tack) the front of the pillow cover to the back. Stitch together using a sewing machine, then remove basting. Trim and notch the seam allowance along the curved edges, and trim away excess fabric from the pointed end of the heart. Turn the cover right side out.

8 Insert the pillow form—you may need to pull the ends of the form around to make sure it fits properly. When it is in position, either hand-stitch the opening closed or sew on ribbon ties and tie these in a neat bow to finish.

picnic basket & rug

For a gift that will be kept and used through the years, line a traditional woven basket to create this delightful picnic basket.

you will need

Pencil and paper for copying template

1¼yd. (1m) of 55in. (137cm) wide printed fabric

Scissors

2¼yd. (2m) gingham ribbon

Needle and thread

Sewing machine

2 snap fasteners

2 buttons ½in. (12mm) in diameter

to line the basket

1 Copy the inside pocket template on page 120 onto paper and cut out. Pin the pattern to the fabric and cut out. To make the base of the basket lining, lay the basket on the fabric and draw around the base, adding ⅞in. (2cm) all around for the seam allowance. For the main basket lining, measure the circumference and height of the basket and add 1¼in. (3cm) seam allowance to each. Cut a piece of fabric to these measurements.

2 Turn the top of the lining under by ⅝in. (15mm) and press flat. Baste (tack) gingham ribbon along this line and topstitch in place along both edges using a sewing machine. Turn under ⅝in. (15mm) along all edges of the pocket and press flat. Baste ribbon along the top edge and topstitch in place as before. Baste the pocket to the main lining approx. 2in. (5cm) down from the top edge. Topstitch the pocket in place, leaving the top edge open. Remove all basting stitches.

3 Stitch one half of both snap fasteners to the inside of the pocket at the top edge, approx. 2in. (5cm) from each end. Stitch the other half of each fastener onto the lining to correspond with the two on the pocket. Stitch two small buttons onto the gingham ribbon to conceal the stitching of the snap fasteners.

4 With right sides facing, machine stitch the side seam of the bag lining, making sure that the ribbon ends at the top edge align. Press the seam flat. With right sides facing, stitch the bag lining to the base section, making small pleats in the fabric if necessary for a proper fit. Trim and notch the seam allowances on the curved edges. Hand-stitch the bag lining to the inside top edge of the basket, using strong thread.

to make the picnic rug

This cozy picnic rug is made from extra-wide fleece fabric and bound in cotton fabric to match the lining of the picnic basket.

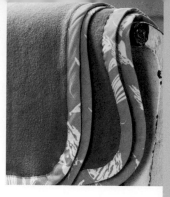

you will need

1⅝yd. (1.5m) of 60in. (150cm) wide fleece fabric

Scissors

28in. (70cm) of 55in. (137cm) wide printed fabric

Sewing machine

Needle and thread

1 Use the scissors to cut all the corners of the fleece square into curves—this makes it much easier to stitch the bias fabric strip around the edges smoothly.

2 Fold the cut end of the cotton fabric to the selvage to form a triangle shape to establish the exact diagonal line. To make the bias strip, cut 2in. (5cm) wide lengths of fabric on the diagonal line of the fabric. Cut sufficient length of bias strip to fit around the four sides of the rug. Join the fabric strips, right sides together, using a sewing machine to achieve the required length.

3 Fold the bias strip in half lengthwise and press flat. Turn the top and bottom edges of the strip under by ⅜in. (10mm) and press flat. Baste (tack) the bias binding in place around the edges of the blanket, making sure that the curved corners of the blanket are neatly sandwiched between the two layers of bias strip.

4 When you have finished basting the bias strip around the blanket, fold the two raw ends to the inside and baste them in place. Use a medium-width zigzag stitch on the sewing machine to stitch the bias strip in place all around. Remove the basting stitches to finish.

tip

Use any remnants of fabric to trim beach towels to match the lined basket, or cut out some of the printed shapes to use as appliqué motifs.

beaded photo album

Cover a plain photo album in pure silk embellished with a band of beaded braid to create a stunning wedding gift, which the happy couple can fill with pictures of their special day.

1 Lay the album flat out with the spine open on the fabric and cut out the fabric covering for the album, adding an extra 2in. (5cm) to each side of the fabric. Pin the braid to the fabric in the center along the longest length of the fabric, and baste (tack) in place. Topstitch the braid in place along both edges using a sewing machine and trim away any loose thread ends with scissors. Remove all basting stitches.

2 Press the reverse of the fabric lightly with a warm iron. Stitch bugle beads to the top and bottom edges of the beaded braid, using a fine needle and thread.

3 Lay the spine of the album along the center of the fabric. Make small cuts in the fabric from the outside edge of the fabric to either side of the spine. Repeat at the other end of the spine.

4 Apply a dab of fabric glue to the center strip of fabric and gently push it up into the spine of the album using the end of your scissors or a pencil. Repeat at the other end of the spine, then allow the glue to dry.

5 Open the album flat and fold the raw fabric corners at the center to the inside to form a triangle, applying a dab of glue to hold in place. Repeat at the other end of the spine and allow the glue to dry.

6 Stand the album with the spine and one side flat and the other side upright. Fold the fabric to the inside of the book on the top edge and glue in position. Repeat on the bottom edge and then cover the other side of the album in the same way.

7 At the outer corners, fold the fabric down to form a neat triangle and then fold the fabric over the edge of the album and glue in position along the edge of the album.

8 Cut the two sheets of paper to fit the inside of the album, with ⅜in. (10mm) trimmed from the three outside edges so the paper is smaller than the album. Cut the grosgrain ribbon in half and glue one piece to the inside of the album where the braid is turned to the inside. Repeat on the other side. Glue the paper to the inside of the album at the front and back to cover the raw fabric edges.

variation

Cover the album and a coordinating presentation box in pure white silk to create a really fabulous gift for a wedding or an anniversary—you could even use the same silk as the wedding or bridesmaid's dress if you have an offcut.

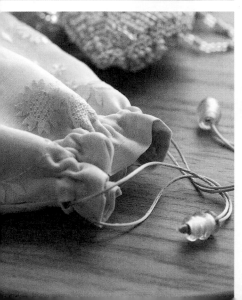

chapter 3
for the girls

Create deliciously feminine gifts for female friends and family, including the prettiest jewelry using glass beads and buttons, stunning beaded candle votives, and lavender-filled hearts stitched from vintage embroidered linens. Made in white silk, the beaded evening bag with sheer ribbon ties would be a stunning gift for a bride. The handmade gifts in this chapter would also make perfect presents for birthdays and Christmas as well as for Mother's Day, or even a bridal shower.

lavender hearts

Vintage embroidered tablecloths and napkins are given a new lease of life as fragrant lavender-filled hearts. Decorate with ribbon bows match colors in the embroidery to create that one-of-a-kind gift.

you will need

Pencil and paper for copying template

Scissors

Pins

Pieces of vintage embroidered cloth

6in. (15cm) square floral fabric for back of heart

Sewing machine

Needle and thread

Spoon

Dried lavender

6in. (15cm) of ⅝in. (15mm) wide ribbon

1 Copy the heart motif from page 121 onto paper and cut out with scissors. Pin the pattern to the vintage embroidered fabric, with the heart centered over a stitched motif. Cut out one heart for the front. Cut another heart for the back from the floral printed fabric.

2 Baste (tack) or pin the hearts together with right sides facing and then stitch together with a sewing machine or by hand, leaving an opening of approx. 1¼in. (3cm) at the top of the heart to add the dried lavender filling. Trim and notch the seam allowances along all the curved edges and remove all bastitng stitches.

3 Turn the fabric heart right sides out and press flat. Use a spoon to fill the heart with the loose dried lavender until it is plump and firm.

4 Hand-stitch to close the opening at the top of the heart. Make a ribbon bow, and trim the ends diagonally with scissors to prevent them from fraying. Hand-stitch the bow to the top of the heart to finish.

tip

Look out for embroidered tablecloths and napkins at thrift stores and secondhand fairs—many of them feature beautiful and decorative embroidery.

friendship bracelet

This pretty bracelet is so simple to make; it's just decorative buttons and sparkling glass beads threaded onto narrow cord. It would make the perfect gift for a dear friend.

you will need

12in. (30cm) narrow cord or ribbon

9 decorative or pearl buttons approx. ½in. (12mm) in diameter

11 small glass beads

Scissors

1 Thread one end of the cord through one hole in the button from the back through to the front.

2 Thread one of the glass beads onto the cord and then thread the end through the second hole to the back of the button. Pull the cord tight so the glass bead lies as flat as possible.

3 Continue threading the buttons with a glass bead on each until you have threaded all nine buttons. Adjust the buttons to overlap each other slightly so that they lie almost flat in a row.

4 Thread a glass bead onto one end of the cord approx. 4in. (10cm) from the end of the first button and then knot the cord. Use scissors to trim the end of the cord down to about ⅜in. (10mm) after the knot. Repeat at the other end of the bracelet.

tip

Look out for highly decorative buttons on items at thrift stores—it's always possible to remove and recycle interesting buttons.

ring of roses basket

A plain oval basket painted hot pink and decorated with rosebuds and daisies makes a delightfully feminine container for a set of rose-scented toiletries. A few fresh flowers add a touch of extra luxury.

1 Paint the basket with undercoat and let dry. Paint the top coat using the pink paint and allow to dry thoroughly. For better coverage of color, apply a second coat of pink.

2 Bend the wire to form the handle. Push the wire ends down into the sides of the basket and add a dab of glue from the glue gun to secure. Using the glue gun, stick daisy braid along the top edge of the wire handle, working on a short length at a time so that the hot glue does not dry too quickly.

3 Stick the white braid around the rim of the basket using the hot glue gun. As with the handle, it is easier to apply glue to short lengths of ribbon and work around the basket slowly in sections so that the hot glue does not dry too quickly.

4 Use craft glue to stick individual roses onto the braid approx. 1¼in. (3cm) apart. Press down firmly to make sure they are securely fixed to the braid. Line the basket with tissue paper and fill with scented toiletries and fresh roses to finish.

tip

Notions sections of department stores or sewing stores are real treasure-troves of decorative trims and ribbons to inspire alternative basket ideas.

candle votives

This glittering glass votive is so quick and simple to make that you could easily create a whole set. Stand them in a row, or dot several around for a stunning effect at an evening garden party.

you will need

Strong clear glue

Paintbrush

Glass tumbler or votive

Clear or silver glass rocaille and bugle beads

Paper plate

12in. (30cm) of ⅛in. (3mm) wide braid or decorative ribbon

Scissors

1 Paint a band of glue approx. ⅞in. (2cm) deep around the top edge of the glass. You may find it easier to do this in sections of about 2in. (5cm) at a time, working your way around the rim of the glass.

2 Mix the beads up on a paper plate. Gently roll the top section of the glass into the mixture, pressing down so that the beads stick to the glue. Repeat until the whole rim of the glass is covered evenly with beads. Allow the glue to dry completely.

3 When the glue is completely dry, use a paintbrush to apply another layer of the glue on top of the beads. This will fix them securely in place and prevent them from falling off. Allow to dry completely again.

4 Wrap the length of braid around the base of the glass and tie in a small bow. Use scissors to trim the ends of the braid to length, cutting diagonally to prevent them from fraying.

tip

Make three or four matching votives and fill with scented tealights to dress a dining table.

gardener's gift

A practical gift for the keen gardener, this wooden basket, which holds handy gardening goodies, is ideal for regular use afterward when cutting flowers. The basket and pots are decorated with a pretty stencil of flowers and leaves.

1 Paint the whole wood basket (including the underside of the base) with white undercoat and allow it to dry thoroughly. If required for better coverage, apply a second coat of undercoat.

2 Paint the handle and outer sides of the basket brown, and let dry. If you wish, use masking tape along the top edges of the basket to make it easier to keep a neat line on the inside.

3 Paint the inside of the basket in pink and let dry completely. You may need to use two coats if it is a very pale color to achieve a really even coverage.

4 Position the stencil on one side of the basket, with masking tape at each corner to hold it in place. Use the stencil brush in an up-and-down stippling motion to apply pink paint through the stencil. Let dry. Repeat the stencil design around all the sides. Seal the basket with two coats of varnish to make it weatherproof.

tip
Traditional wooden baskets—or trugs—are often available from garden centers, craft stores, or online suppliers (see page 127 for addresses).

5 Paint the outside of both terracotta pots and the upper half of the inside of each pot with white undercoat. Allow to dry completely.

6 Apply pink paint to the outside of one pot, leaving the top rim unpainted so that it can be decorated in the contrasting color. Let dry thoroughly.

7 Paint the rim of the pot in the contrasting color and let dry. Use the same color to paint the upper half of the inside of the pot. Paint the second pot, swapping the position of the colors so that you end up with two contrasting pots.

8 Place the stencil on the front of the pot and secure in place with masking tape at each corner. Apply contrasting color paint using a stencil brush as before and let dry. Carefully remove the stencil and then repeat on the other pot. Place the pots and other gardening gifts into the basket.

variation

To make a similar gift for someone with no garden, just paint a set of several coordinating pots to stand in a line planted with pretty flowers. Alternatively, stencil each pot with the name of a herb and plant up with the corresponding herb for the perfect kitchen display.

spring bulb planter

A basket planted with flowering spring bulbs is a fragrant and welcome gift for display indoors or out. When the bulbs have finished flowering, they can be planted in the garden, to bring back memories of the gift each spring.

you will need

Basket with handle

White undercoat

Paintbrush

Green paint

Waterproof varnish

Plastic sheeting

Double-sided tape

1¼yd. (1m) of ⅝in. (15mm) wide gingham ribbon in blue and in yellow

Scissors

Hot glue gun

Potting compost

Flowering bulbs

1 Apply white undercoat to the basket and let dry completely. Apply one or two coats of the green paint and let dry. Finish with a coat of waterproof varnish, particularly if the basket Is to be used outside.

2 Cut the plastic sheeting to fit the inside of the basket, allowing approx. 1½in. (4cm) extra on all edges to fold inside. Fix the folded top edge of the plastic to the rim of the basket using double-sided tape.

3 Tie the gingham ribbon into bows and cut the ends diagonally using scissors to prevent fraying. Use a hot glue gun to stick the blue and yellow ribbon bows alternately around the edge of the basket.

4 Fill the base of the basket with potting compost and plant the bulbs inside. Fill the gaps between the bulbs with more compost and press down firmly to ensure the bulbs stay upright. Water very sparingly.

tip

The stems of tall bulbs, such as these hyacinths, can bend under the weight of the flowerheads, so support them with short, thin, wooden plant stakes.

evening bag

This dainty evening bag is decorated with tiny rocaille beads and lined with a charming vintage silk scarf.

you will need

Paper and pencil for copying template

Scissors

Pins

8 x 20in. (20 x 50cm) of fabric

8 x 20in. (20 x 50cm) of lining fabric

Gold rocaille beads

Needle and thread

Sewing machine

32in. (80cm) of ⅜in. (10mm) wide sheer ribbon for drawstring

Safety pin

2 large glass beads

Glue

1 Copy the evening bag template on page 120 onto paper and cut out with scissors. Pin the pattern to the fabric and cut out two bag pieces from the main fabric and two from the lining fabric.

2 Stitch the rocaille beads to the main fabric according to the design of the fabric. This bag is in an embroidered fabric but if you choose to use a printed fabric, stitch the beads around the motifs. Repeat on both pieces of the main fabric.

3 With right sides facing, baste (tack) the two pieces of fabric together, leaving the top (straight edge) of the bag open as well as leaving a ⅝in. (15mm) opening on each side of the bag approx. 1¾in. (4.5cm) down from the top. Repeat for the lining fabric, but omit the side openings. Use a sewing machine to stitch around the edges of the bag and the bag lining. Remove all basting stitches.

4 Trim and notch the seam allowances on the curved edges. Turn the main bag fabric right side out and press the stitched seams gently.

tip

Check remnant boxes in fabric stores for small pieces of decorative fabric at reduced prices, which will be perfect for making this small evening bag.

5 Insert the bag lining into the bag and fold the raw edges of the fabric over to the inside by ⅜in. (10mm). Baste (tack) the lining to the bag fabric around the top opening.

6 Topstitch around the edge approx. ⅜in. (10mm) in from the fold, then remove the basting stitches. Press the edges of the bag with a warm iron. Next, work two rows of topstitching around the bag at approx. ⅞in. (2cm) from the top and 1¼in. (3cm) from the top—these lines of stitching need to fall on either side of the gaps left in the side seams in step 3. They will form the casing for the ribbon drawstring, which is inserted through the gaps.

7 Cut the ribbon in half. Insert the safety pin through one end and thread a length of ribbon through one opening in the bag, right around and out again. Thread the other piece of ribbon through the other side of the bag in the same way.

8 Thread the two ribbon ends on one side of the bag through a large bead and tie in a knot. Trim the ribbon ends and add a dab of glue to the knot to keep it in place at the end of the bead. Repeat with the ends on the other side of the bag.

variation

If you were to make this little bag In cream or white fabric with crystal beads, it would be perfect for bridesmaids to carry at a wedding. Alternatively, you could make several bags in different colors and fabrics to match your favorite evening dresses.

chapter 4
at home

These gifts make ideal offerings for homemakers—perhaps to mark the purchase of a new home or simply as a thank-you token for your host after a special occasion. The projects include a delicately stenciled tray using paper doilies, vintage teacups turned into unusual candles, a brightly colored pillow decorated with beading, embroidery, and felt flowers, and pretty fabric bunting to hang in a child's bedroom. All the projects would work equally well in different colors and fabrics, and can be adapted to suit different tastes and age groups.

new home card

By using a thick needle to create a graphic punched design, you can create this stylish greetings card for a new homeowner. It would be ideal to hold a gift card for a home store.

you will need

Paper and pencil for copying template

Scissors

Blank greetings card with envelope

Piece of foam or polystyrene

Thick sewing needle

Soft eraser

Glue

Heart-shaped button

6in. (15cm) of ⅜in. (10mm) wide ribbon

1 Copy the house template on page 119 onto paper and cut out. Use a soft pencil to draw around the pattern onto the front of the blank card and then draw in the windows and door.

2 Open the greetings card and place the front over a piece of foam or polystyrene. Use the needle to pierce holes along all the drawn lines, spacing them approx. ⅟₁₆in. (1–2mm) apart.

3 Use a soft eraser to remove the remaining pencil lines. Stick the heart-shaped button to the card below the house with a dab of glue, and let dry.

4 Make a small bow in gingham ribbon. Trim the ends diagonally to prevent them from fraying. Glue the bow to the card above the button and let dry fully. You could also add a matching bow to the back of the envelope flap.

tip

Stick a piece of colored tissue paper behind the pierced design for extra decorative effect.

fabric
bunting

Make this fun floral and gingham fabric bunting
to decorate the garden for a party or to hang in
a child's bedroom. It's a great way to use up larger
scraps of fabric—and smaller scraps are ideal for
the Patchwork Teapot Cozy on page 78.

you will need

Paper and pencil for
copying template

Scissors

Pins

6 x 8in. (15 x 20cm) per
triangle of assorted floral
and checked fabrics

Pinking shears

Sewing machine

Safety pin

Several yards (meters) of
⅛in. (3mm) wide ribbon

1 Copy the bunting template
on page 125 onto paper and
cut out. Pin the pattern to a
piece of fabric and cut out
the bunting shapes, using
pinking shears to prevent the
fabric edges from fraying.
Repeat until you have
enough bunting triangles.

2 Fold the side (angled)
edges of one triangle over
by ⅜in. (10mm) to the wrong
side of the fabric and pin in
place. Press these edges flat
and topstitch in place using
a sewing machine. Repeat
for all the bunting triangles.

3 Fold the straight top edge
of each triangle over by ⅝in.
(15mm) to the wrong side of
the fabric, pin in place, and
press flat. Repeat for each
triangle and then topstitch
the edges in place to create
the ribbon casing.

4 Attach the safety pin to
one end of the ribbon and
thread through the casing on
each triangle in turn, leaving
a gap of approximately
1½–2in. (4–5cm) between
each. You can make a small
stitch through the center of
each flag to hold it in place
on the ribbon if you prefer.
Leave around 8in. (20cm) of
ribbon free at each end for
fixing the bunting in place.

tip

Try using printed paper to create cheap and colorful
bunting—you can even use paper doilies threaded onto
white ribbon to create a delicate, lace-effect bunting for
a wedding or christening.

wax candle cups

These teacup candles would make a pretty table centerpiece in a selection of different vintage cups and saucers. Try using different fragrances of wax to create your own scented candles.

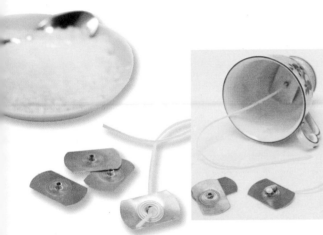

1 Thread the wick through the metal end piece and tie a knot. Measure the depth of the cup, add approx. 2in. (5cm), and trim the wick to match this measurement.

2 Use a small piece of adhesive putty to fix the metal end piece to the bottom of a cup. Press firmly in place.

3 Gently wrap the excess wick around the popsicle (lolly) stick so that the wick stands upright in the cup. Balance the popsicle (lolly) stick on the rim of the cup to keep the wick in position while the wax is poured and cools. Melt the wax beads on a low heat in the saucepan. Pour the wax into the cup to approx. ⅜in. (10mm) below the rim.

4 Allow the wax to cool and solidify completely. Use the scissors to trim the wick, leaving a length of about ⅞in. (2cm) standing above the top of the wax.

tip

Use old candles to make new ones by melting them in an old saucepan—you can buy wax color dyes and fragrances to add during the melting process.

patchwork teapot cozy

As well as being a great way to use up small pieces of fabric, patchwork is a soothing and enjoyable pastime. This cheerful teapot cozy is made of hexagonal patches in red and white patterned fabrics, finished with a decorative fringed braid.

you will need

Pencil and paper for copying templates

Thin cardstock

Scissors

Scraps of red and white cotton fabric

Pins

Needle and thread

15in. (40cm) square of lightweight batting (wadding)

18in. (45cm) of 55in. (137cm) wide lining fabric

Sewing machine

24in. (60cm) ruffled fabric braid

2½in. (6cm) of ⅜in. (10mm) wide gingham ribbon

8in. (20cm) of ⅞in. (2cm) wide spotty ribbon

1 Copy the templates for the paper and fabric hexagons on page 122 and transfer onto thin cardstock. Copy the teapot cozy shape onto paper. Cut them out. Draw around the fabric hexagon pattern to make approx. 120 fabric hexagons. Use the paper hexagon pattern to make the same number of paper hexagons.

2 Place a paper hexagon on the wrong side of a fabric hexagon, making sure it is in the center. Fold one fabric edge over the paper and baste (tack) to hold in place. Continue to fold fabric edges over until they are all basted (tacked) into position. Repeat for all the fabric hexagons.

3 Place two hexagons right sides facing and whipstitch together along one edge. Add hexagons along the other edges in the same way. Alternate fabric designs as you work so that the same fabric pattern is not repeated in adjacent hexagons.

4 Continue stitching hexagons together to make a patchwork fabric. Lay the patchwork over the teapot cozy pattern to see where you need more patches—the piece of patchwork should overlap the pattern by ⅜–⅝in. (10–15mm) all around. When it is big enough, make a second piece for the back of the cozy. When both pieces are finished, remove the basting (tacking) and the patchwork papers.

5 Use the teapot cozy pattern to cut out two pieces of batting (wadding) and of lining fabric. Place the two layers of patchwork right sides facing, add one layer of batting (wadding) on each side, and pin in place.

6 Machine-stitch the four layers together. Trim and notch the seam allowances on curved edges and turn the teapot cozy right sides out. Press using a hot iron.

7 With right sides facing, machine-stitch the two layers of lining fabric together along the curved edge. Trim and notch seam allowances, then insert the lining fabric inside the cozy. Pin the bottom edges together and then topstitch. Finish raw edges with zigzag stitching to prevent them from fraying.

8 Pin the ruffled braid along the bottom edge of the cozy and hand-stitch in place. Make a loop in gingham ribbon and stitch to the top of the cozy. Tie the spot ribbon into a bow, trim the ends diagonally to prevent fraying, and stitch to cover the raw ends of the gingham loop.

tip

Wash all the fabrics together beforehand because they may have different shrinkage rates, which can cause patchwork to pucker when washed later.

variation

Patchwork motifs can be used as appliqué to give a whole new look to a plain pillow cover, or even to a simple patterned one, as shown here. This flower is made up of just seven hexagons joined together, with two diamond shapes for the leaves (there is a template for the leaves on page 122). Embroider the stem in either stem stitch or chain stitch.

stenciled wooden tray

Paper doilies feature pretty lacy designs that are perfect for stenciling. This simple wooden tray comes alive by adding zingy color and a delicate rectangular lace design over the base.

you will need

Plain wooden tray
White undercoat
Paintbrush
Green and white paint
Paper lace doily
Masking tape
Stencil brush
Paper towels
White lace self-adhesive paper ribbon
Water-based acrylic varnish

1 Paint the top of the tray in white undercoat and let dry. Turn the tray over and paint the underside, and then let dry completely. Paint the tray with the main paint color in the same way. Add a second coat of paint if required for complete coverage. Let the painted tray dry completely.

2 Lay the doily in position on the tray. Stick a border of masking tape around the doily approx. ¼in. (6mm) away from the edge. Dip the stencil brush in white paint and remove the excess by wiping on paper towels— this prevents paint from bleeding under the stencil. Apply paint over the whole of the stencil and up to the edge of the masking tape.

3 When the stencil paint is almost dry, remove the strips of masking tape very carefully. Lift the doily stencil from one corner of the tray and peel back carefully to reveal the whole stenciled motif.

4 Peel back the self-adhesive backing from the paper ribbon and stick it to the outer side of the tray approx. ³⁄₁₆in. (4mm) up from the bottom. Apply a coat of water-based acrylic varnish over the whole tray and allow to dry completely before use.

tip

Use circular paper doilies to stencil place mats and look out for tiny doilies to make stenciled coasters.

decoupage coasters

Old maps add a new look to plain coasters—personalize your gift by using maps of places that mean something to the recipient. See page 36 for a matching picture frame.

you will need

Blank wooden coasters

White undercoat

Paintbrush

Blue paint

Copyright-free map images

Mug or a pair of compasses

Pencil

Scalpel or scissors

Glue

Water-based acrylic varnish

1 Paint the top and side edges of each coaster with white undercoat and let dry. Apply undercoat to the other side of the coasters and allow to dry completely.

2 Apply the blue paint to the top and sides of the coasters and let dry. Repeat on the underside and let dry completely. Add a second coat if required.

3 Use a mug to match the size of the coaster or a pair of compasses to mark circular shapes on interesting areas of the map. Cut out the circle shapes using a scalpel or scissors.

4 Apply a thin layer of glue over the back of a map circle and stick it to a coaster. Press flat all over to remove any air bubbles. Repeat for each of the other coasters. When completely dry, apply one coat of water-based acrylic varnish.

tip

Use larger map sections to make matching place mats for the coasters. Remember to seal the paper against spills with a thin layer of varnish.

embroidered pillow

Fabric flowers, beads, and embroidery can all be added to a flower-print pillow cover to give it a subtle 3-D effect and a touch of glamorous sparkle.

you will need

18in. (45cm) of 55in. (137cm) wide floral fabric

Scissors

14 x 22in. (35 x 55cm) piece of lightweight batting (wadding)

Pins

Needle and thread

5–6 felt flowers

Blue and gold glass beads

Green embroidery floss

Sewing machine

4 snap fasteners

12 x 20in. (30 x 50cm) pillow form

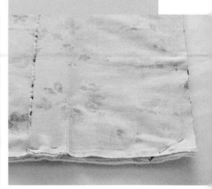

1 Cut out one rectangle of fabric measuring 13¼in x 21¼in. (33 x 53cm) for the front and two rectangles of fabric 8½ x 21¼in. (22 x 53cm) for the back. Cut out a piece of batting (wadding) 13¼in x 21¼in. (33 x 53cm) and pin to the wrong side of the main rectangle of fabric. Baste (tack) in place ready for the embroidery and other decoration.

2 Hand-stitch the felt flowers onto the fabric over some of the flower prints, scattering them across the area equally. Stitch a blue glass bead at the center of each felt flower.

3 Stitch blue and gold glass beads at the center of some printed flowers. Use three strands of six-strand embroidery floss to work leaves in long running stitch in groups of three stitches around the felt flowers.

4 Fold a long edge of one back piece to the wrong side by 1¾in. (4.5cm) and press. Lay this piece right sides facing on the front piece with the fold in the center, then lay the other back piece on top with the wrong side uppermost. Pin in place. Machine stitch around the edge to join back and front together, then remove the basting stitches. Insert the pillow form. Hand-stitch the snap fasteners to the sides of the back opening.

tip

Look out for decorative fabric prints that would look good with added beads and embroidery—cotton fabrics work best for this project.

beaded throw

This elegant throw would make a stylish and decorative addition to any plain sofa or armchair. Look out for interesting beaded braid to trim your throw in the notions or haberdashery section of department stores and craft stores.

you will need

20 x 48in. (50 x 120cm) piece of fabric

Pins

Scissors

Needle and thread

22in. (55cm) length of beaded braid

Sewing machine

22in. (55cm) length of beaded fringing

Rocaille beads

Small plastic faceted beads

1 On the top and bottom raw edges of the fabric, make a double hem by folding over the edge twice by ⅜in. (10mm) each time. Pin in place.

2 Baste (tack) the top hem using large running stitches. Repeat for the other hem. Gently press both hems flat when all the sewing is complete.

3 Pin the beaded braid to the bottom of the throw approx. 2in. (5cm) in from the edge. Baste (tack) the braid along both edges and then remove all the pins.

4 Topstitch along both edges of the beaded braid using the sewing machine. Remove any basting (tacking) stitches and press the throw lightly with a warm iron on the reverse of the fabric.

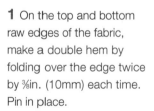

tip

You could use a readymade shawl or throw for this project. Measure the hem to work out the lengths of beaded braid and fringing required, adding ⅞in. (2cm) to these measurements for hems.

5 Pin the beaded fringing to the wrong side of the throw, along the basted (tacked) hem. Baste (tack) in position using small stitches. Remove the pins before machine-stitching.

6 Carefully machine-stitch the fringing to the throw, making sure that the beads do not get caught up as you work—use your hands to guide the fringing away from the needle. Remove the basting (tacking) stitches.

7 Using doubled thread in a needle, stitch a row of rocaille beads approx. ⅜in. (10mm) apart alongside the beaded braid and about ⅜in. (10mm) away from the edge. Repeat on the other side of the braid.

8 On the side edges of the throw, make a double hem by folding over the edge twice by ⅜in. (10mm) each time. Pin the hem in place. Stitch a row of plastic faceted beads approx. ⅝in. (15mm) apart along each edge of the throw to hold the hem in position.

variation

This design made in a lightweight silk would make the most luxurious evening wrap to wear around the shoulders. For this you will have to repeat the beaded braid and fringing at both ends of the wrap, so you will need double the quantity of braid and fringing given.

chapter 5
babies & children

The gifts in this chapter are for babies and children; the baby basket would be the perfect present for a newborn, while the painted wood letters could be decorated to mark a christening or a birthday. Use different colors and fabrics to adapt the ideas to suit a boy or girl, or use neutral colors and patterns if the sex of the baby is not yet known. Children will enjoy making some of the simpler projects in this chapter themselves—such as the pompom bag or painted letters, which they can then give to friends or family members.

appliqué blanket

This warm and cuddly blanket is decorated with a colorful motif of cars and finished with contrasting blanket stitching. It's sure to win the heart of any child and will quickly become a bedtime essential.

you will need

Paper and pencil for copying templates

Scissors

Pins

12in. (30cm) squares of assorted gingham fabrics

12in. (30cm) square of black cotton fabric

12in. (30cm) squares of fusible web

1¾yd. (1.5m) square of blanket fabric

Sewing machine

Wool yarn and needle

1 Copy the car, wheel, and window templates on page 123 onto paper and cut out. Iron fusible web onto the back of all the gingham and black fabric squares. Transfer the car outline onto the backing paper of the fusible web on the reverse of the gingham fabrics. You will need four cars in each color of gingham fabric.

2 Transfer the wheel and window shapes onto the backing paper of the fusible web on the reverse of the black fabric. You will need two wheels and two window shapes for each car.

3 Lay the cars along the edges of the blanket fabric at even intervals, alternating colors. Pin each one in position. Lift each car separately, peel the backing paper off, and iron in position on the blanket fabric. Repeat until all the cars are fixed. Peel the backing paper away from the windows and wheels, and iron these to each car shape using the photograph above as a guide.

tip

You could use a readymade blanket to appliqué, which would save time as you wouldn't have to do any blanket stitch. Make cushions to match with larger car motifs—use a photocopier to enlarge the templates.

4 With cotton to match the blanket color in the sewing machine, work a narrow zigzag stitch around the car and wheels. Work the same zigzag stitch around the windows. Trim any loose ends of thread with scissors.

5 Use a wider and closer zigzag stitch to fill in the space between the two car windows. Trim the thread ends with scissors. When you have finished sewing all the car motifs, press the back of each motif on the reverse of the blanket fabric with a warm iron.

6 Use scissors to cut each of the corners of the blanket into a gentle curve to make it easier to work the blanket stitch around the corners.

7 Fold over the edges of the blanket to the wrong side by approx. ½in. (12mm) and pin in place. Baste (tack) the hem in place and press.

8 Using contrasting yarn and a thick needle, work blanket stitch around all the edges of the blanket. Fasten off at the end neatly. Press the blanket stitching on the reverse of the fabric using a warm iron.

variation

Make the same blanket in more feminine colors for a little girl, and add an appliqué flower (see page 123) instead of the car. You could also appliqué the child's name or initials, or use suitable motifs cut from printed fabrics.

baby basket

This decorative woven basket can be filled with towels, blankets, and clothes to create the perfect offering for a baby shower or gift for a newborn baby. Afterward, it will be ideal to store all those essential everyday baby items, such as diapers, a change mat, and clothes such as socks and bibs.

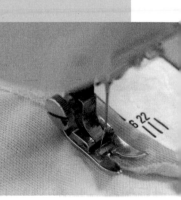

1 Copy the lining template on page 124 onto paper, sized to fit the height and width of the basket, and cut out. The curved section on the sides makes it easier to fold the fabric over the top. Pin the pattern to the fabric and cut out four pieces of fabric.

2 Place two pieces of fabric for the sides of the basket, right sides facing, and machine-stitch together. Repeat until all four sides are joined. Notch seam allowances on the curved edges at the top of the lining.

3 Cut out a piece of fabric to fit the base of the basket. Using scissors, gently curve the corners of the base fabric, which will make it easier to sew the sides on at the corners. Baste (tack) the four-piece side section to the base with right sides together and then machine-stitch the seams. Notch seam allowances on the curved edges. Remove the basting (tacking) stitches.

4 Zigzag-stitch along the raw edges, then turn them over by approx. ⅜in. (10mm) and press flat. Stitch in place as close to the bottom edge of the fabric as possible to make the casing for the elastic, leaving an opening of approx. ⅝in. (15mm) in the stitching to insert the elastic.

tip

The template can be adapted to fit your basket by cutting it to measure the height of the basket to the start of the curved section by the width of the sides of the basket plus ⅞in. (2cm) for seams.

variation

If you don't know whether the new baby will be a boy or a girl, make the baby basket in neutral colors, as shown in this smart oatmeal linen variation, or in pretty shades of soft yellow, mint green, or classic cream.

5 Attach a safety pin to one end of the elastic and thread the elastic through the casing. When you have finished threading, pull the fabric so it lies almost flat.

6 If required, press the basket lining before fitting it to the basket. Pull the sides of the fabric over the rim of the basket so that it fits neatly, and pull the ends of the elastic together to fit. Tie the elastic in several knots to secure and trim the ends. Hand-stitch the casing opening closed.

7 To make the gift tag for the basket, copy the small heart template on page 124 onto paper and cut out. Draw around the heart onto a scrap of the fabric and cut out with scissors.

8 Spray a thin layer of glue—use adhesive spray in a well-ventilated room—over the back of the fabric heart. Glue the heart to the front of the tag and then let dry completely.

baby towel & facecloth set

This cute towel and facecloth set is decorated with a sailboat motif and edged in bright bias tape. Cutting motifs from printed fabric is a great way to coordinate with other items in the room.

you will need

1½yd. (1.25m) of 55in. (137cm) wide terrycloth fabric

Scissors

Pencil and paper for copying template

Pins

Fabric motif

Fusible web to fit motif size

Sewing machine

5¼yd. (4.75m) of 1in. (2.5cm) wide bias tape

Needle and thread

to make the towel

1 Cut out a 36in. (90cm) square of terrycloth. Trace the hood template on page 125 onto paper and cut out. Pin the pattern to the leftover piece of terrycloth and cut out one hood section. Lay this over one corner of the terrycloth square and use it to cut a matching curve. Repeat on each corner of the towel.

2 Iron the fusible web to the wrong side of the fabric motif and cut out the design. Peel off the backing paper, then center the motif on the hood triangle and iron in place. Zigzag-stitch with a sewing machine around the edge of the motif.

3 Fold the bias tape in half vertically and press. Cut a length of bias tape to fit the bottom straight edge of the hood. Baste (tack) in place. Stitch the bias tape in place using a sewing machine.

4 Pin the hood to one corner of the towel. Baste (tack) bias tape around the edges of the double fabric section and then continue around all four sides of the towel, taking care on the curved corners. Topstitch along the edge to hold the bias tape in place. Remove the basting (tacking) to finish.

tip

You could substitute ready-made embroidered motifs on this project—these are available from most craft stores and notions sections in department stores.

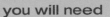

Make this baby facecloth to match the hooded baby towel—as well as the sailboat motif, it features cute sailboat braid along the bottom edge, which makes a handy hanging loop.

to make the facecloth

you will need

Pencil and paper for copying template

12in. (30cm) square of terrycloth fabric

Scissors

10in. (25cm) of ⅜in. (10mm) wide braid

Needle and thread

Fabric motif

Fusible web

Sewing machine

Pins

1yd. (90cm) of 1in. (2.5cm) wide bias tape

1 Trace the facecloth template on page 124 and cut out two facecloth shapes from terrycloth fabric. Baste (tack) the braid to the bottom edge of one facecloth section approx. 1¼in. (3cm) from the edge. Topstitch in place, then remove the basting stitches.

2 Iron fusible web to the back of the fabric motif and then cut out the shape. Peel off the backing paper and iron the motif above the braid on the facecloth. Machine-zigzag around all the edges of the motif to hold it in place.

3 With right sides facing, pin the two facecloth shapes together and then machine-stitch the two pieces together around the curved end and sides, leaving the straight edge at the base open. Finish along the raw edges of the seam allowance with medium zigzag stitch to prevent any excessive fraying.

4 Turn the facecloth right sides out. Fold the bias tape in half vertically and press. Enclose the raw edges around the base of the facecloth in the bias tape. Topstitch in place, folding the raw ends of the bias tape to the inside to finish. Make a loop from the braid and hand-stitch to the facecloth at one corner.

tip

You could embroider the baby's initials on the facecloth instead of using a fabric motif. Work this in chain stitch with brightly colored embroidery floss.

painted
alphabet

Brightly painted initials or even a whole name make
an eye-catching display in a child's bedroom. Plain
wood letters are available in many sizes and fonts
for you to decorate as you choose.

you will need

Selection of plain wood
letters

White undercoat

Thick and fine
paintbrushes

Various colors of main
paint

Ruler

Pencil

Pair of compasses or
suitable circle shape

1 Apply a layer of white
undercoat to the front of
each letter and let dry. Paint
the back of the letter and let
dry completely.

2 Paint the letter in the main
base color and let dry
completely. If necessary,
apply a second coat for
complete coverage.

3 Use a ruler and pencil
to draw out the lines for the
painted stripes, spaced
approx. 1in. (2.5cm) apart.
Draw in the spots using a
pair of compasses or a
suitable circle shape.

4 Fill in the stripes or spots
using a fine paintbrush and
let dry. You may find it faster
to paint the outline edge
using the fine brush and
then fill in the middle area
using a much thicker brush.

tip

Try decorating the wood letters with stick-on flower motifs
in shades of pink, orange, and red. Seal with clear varnish
to protect the motifs.

stenciled child's chair

A simple stenciled chair will be treasured for years after the child has outgrown it. For a more personalized gift, add the child's initials, name, or the date of birth.

you will need

Plain wood chair
Sandpaper
White undercoat
Paintbrush
Pink and white paints
Stencil
Stencil brush
Paper towels
Water-based acrylic varnish

1 Sand the chair to prepare the surface for painting. Paint it with white undercoat and let dry completely. Apply the main pink color and let dry. Apply a second coat of paint if required for complete coverage and allow to dry completely.

2 Place the stencil in the center of the chair seat. Dip the stencil brush into the white paint and blot on paper towels to remove excess paint. Apply the paint by stippling the brush through the stencil. Allow the paint to dry completely.

3 Carefully lift the stencil to reveal the stenciled design. If any of the paint has leaked through to the reverse of the stencil, wipe off with paper towels or wash the stencil and allow to dry completely before reusing it.

4 Use different areas of the stencil to decorate the bars of the chair, or stencil numbers or letters as required. When the paint is completely dry, add a coat of water-based acrylic varnish to protect the design.

tip

Instead of stenciling, you could decorate the chair with decoupage using favorite nursery motifs. See page 36 for the decoupage technique.

russian dolls

Russian doll blanks are so easy to decorate. They are ideal as a colorful display—or as a unique container for a special gift.

you will need

Set of blank Russian dolls

White undercoat

Medium and fine paintbrushes

Selection of colored paints

Fine pencil

Water-based acrylic varnish

Tiny buttons

3-d fabric paint

Tiny bows

Glue

1 Paint the Russian dolls with white undercoat and let dry. If the wood is very porous, you may need a second coat. Leave the inside rims around the middle of the dolls clear, since painting these makes it difficult to put the top section back on the doll.

2 Apply the main color to the whole doll and let dry completely. Apply a further coat if required. Use a fine pencil to draw in the face and headscarf. Fill in the face using flesh-color paint and then add the eyes and the hair using black paint.

3 Use a fine paintbrush to draw the edges of the headscarf and knot and then use a thicker paintbrush to fill in the whole headscarf. Use red paint for the mouth. Let paint dry completely and then apply a layer of water-based acrylic varnish to protect the design.

4 Decorate the largest doll with tiny buttons and small dots using 3-d fabric paint. Glue a tiny bow to the doll's headscarf. If you want the dolls to continue to nest, add detail with paint only to the remaining dolls.

tip

Look on the Internet for more intricate or traditional designs for your Russian doll blanks—there are many sites depicting exquisite designs.

pompom book bag

Pompoms in pretty shades of mauve and damson have been used to finish this wool bag, but they are suitable for any fabric item. Use several different colors together for a multicolor pompom.

you will need

Two pieces of stiff cardstock

Scissors or craft knife

Mauve and damson light worsted (double knitting) yarn

Sharp scissors

Darning needle

1 Cut out two circles, measuring the diameter you want the pompom, from the pieces of cardstock. Cut out a center circle half the size from each—you may find it easier to use a craft knife rather than scissors. Place the two disks together, thread the end of the yarn through the center hole, and knot. Begin to wind the yarn around the disk, through the center hole each time.

2 Continue winding, giving a gentle tug on the yarn each time to make sure it is tightly bound. To make a really full and tight pompom, you will need to wrap the yarn until the center hole is almost completely filled. When you have finished winding, slide the sharp scissors between the layers of cardstock and cut the strands of yarn all around.

3 Gently ease the two pieces of cardstock apart just a little. Cut a length of yarn approx. 16in. (40cm) long and fold in half. Slide the yarn between the two layers of cardstock and tie into a very tight knot. This will secure the pompom and prevent the yarn strands from falling out, so it is important to tie this as tightly as possible.

4 Use both hands to gently prize the cardstock circles off the pompom and fluff it out. Trim any longer ends to create a perfect ball. Use the ends of the length of yarn to stitch the pompom to a bag or garment, using a darning needle.

felt cellphone case

A young teenage girl would love this cellphone case, made in brightly colored felt and decorated with a plaid (tartan) bow and felt charms.

1 Copy the cellphone case templates on page 121 onto paper and cut out. Pin the case pattern to pink felt and cut out two pieces. Pin the flap pattern to green felt and cut one on the fold. Lay the pink felt pieces flat on top of one another and use cross-stitch to join the two case sections to the fold of the flap. Press flat using a warm iron.

2 Fold the main body of the case in half to form the pocket. Work small blanket stitches approx. ⅛in. (3mm) apart in a contrasting embroidery floss to stitch the side seams and to finish the top seam. Slipstitch blue ribbon around the bottom of the case. Hand-stitch a plastic snap fastener to the underside of the flap and the other half of the fastener to the main piece to match.

3 Thread the two felt charms onto the narrow ribbon and tie a small knot at the end. Stitch the ends of the narrow ribbon securely by hand between the two flaps. Work blanket stitch to stitch the two halves of the flap together in contrasting embroidery floss.

4 Make a bow in plaid (tartan) ribbon and trim the ends diagonally to prevent them from fraying. Stitch or glue the fabric flower to the center of the bow. Use fabric glue to stick the bow to the middle of the flap and let dry completely. Finish with a couple of stitches to make the bow more secure, if necessary.

tip

This case works equally well for an iPod or MP3 player—use the player as a template, adding ⅜in. (10mm) to each side for the seam allowance.

templates

This section includes all the templates you will need for the projects in this book. Some are at full-size and can be traced and used as they are; others are half-size and you will need a photocopier to enlarge them by 200%.

Position of
chandelier droplet

chandelier drop heart

Page 30
This template is at half-size, so photocopy it at 200%.

father's day apron

apron pocket

Page 34
This template is at half-size, so photocopy it at 200%.
NB: The template for the main apron is on page 126.

christmas stocking

stocking cuff

Page 18
This template is at half-size, so photocopy it at 200%.
NB: The template for the main stocking is on page 126.

christmas stocking

stocking embroidery

Page 18
This template is at half-size, so
photocopy it at 200%.

monogrammed pillows

Page 38
Both of the templates for the Monogrammed Pillows are
at half-size, so photocopy them at 200%.

front section

Page 38

back section

Page 38

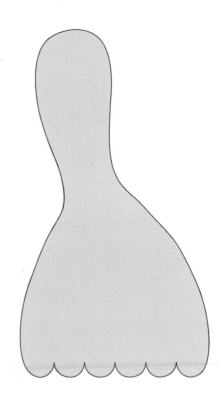

felt egg cozies

Page 14
This template is at half-size, so
photocopy it at 200%.

new home card

Page 72
This template is full-size; trace
and use at this size.

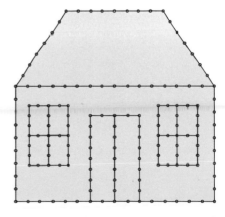

picnic basket

inside pocket

Page 42
This template is at half-size, so
photocopy it at 200%.

evening bag

Page 66
This template is at half-size, so
photocopy it at 200%.

case

Page 114

flap

Page 114

Place to fold of fabric

felt cellphone case

Page 114
Both of the templates for the felt cellphone case
are full-size; trace and use at this size (or adapt to
suit the shape of your phone).

lavender heart

Page 52
This template is at half-size,
so photocopy it at 200%.

patchwork teapot cozy

Page 78
All the templates for the Patchwork
Teapot Cozy are at half-size, so
photocopy them at 200%.

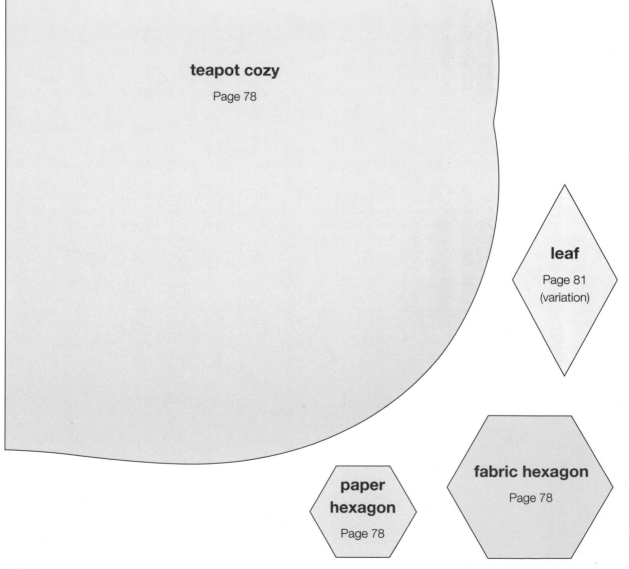

teapot cozy

Page 78

leaf

Page 81
(variation)

fabric hexagon

Page 78

**paper
hexagon**

Page 78

appliqué blanket

Page 94

All the templates for the Appliqué Blanket
are full-size; trace and use at this size.

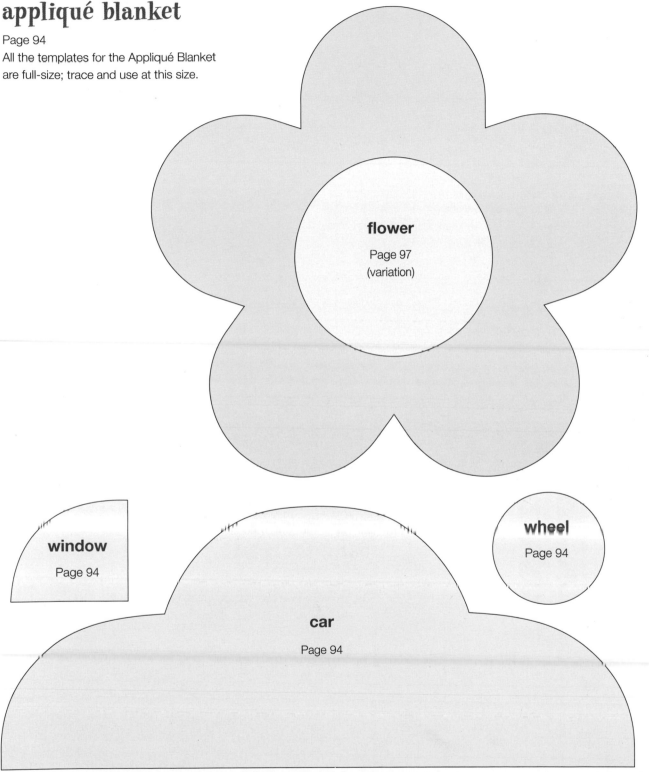

flower

Page 97
(variation)

window

Page 94

wheel

Page 94

car

Page 94

baby basket

lining

Page 98
This template shows how to cut the fabric lining wider at the top, to allow it to fold over the sides of the basket with ease. See the tip box on page 99 for advice on adapting the size to suit your own basket.

baby basket

heart tag

Page 98
This template is full-size; trace and use at this size.

baby facecloth

Page 104
This template is at half-size, so photocopy it at 200%.

fabric bunting

Page 74
This template is at half-size, so
photocopy it at 200%.

baby towel

hood

Page 102
This template is at half-size, so photocopy
it at 200%.

The grid below indicates the size of these templates—each square equals 2in. (5cm). Draw these up to the full-sizes on paper. You may find it easier to use squared pattern paper to do this (available from sewing supplies stores and online retailers—see opposite).

5in. (12.5cm)

father's day apron

Page 34
Cut one to fold of fabric.

christmas stocking

Page 18

9in. (23cm)

Position of embroidered Christmas tree

23in. (58cm)

35in. (88cm)

Place to fold of fabric

24in. (61cm)

12½in. (31.5cm)

13in. (33cm)

useful addresses

USA/Canada

A. C. Moore
Tel: +1 888 226 6673
www.acmoore.com
Vast selection of arts, crafts, and floral merchandise.

ArtSuppliesOnline
Tel: +1 800 967 7367/+1 612 333 3330
www.artsuppliesonline.com
Art and craft supplies.

Art Cove
Tel: +1 718 381 7782
www.artcove.com
Wide range of arts and crafts supplies.

Arts Crafts USA
Tel: +1 301 379 7126
www.artscraftsusa.com
Embroidery and other craft supplies.

BJ's Craft Supplies
Tel: +1 361 286 3181
www.bjcraftsupplies.com
General craft supplies, including beads, sequins, and sewing materials.

Butterick
www.butterick.com
Supplier of pattern paper and other sewing equipment.

C and J Craft Supply
Tel: +1 800 833 4788
www.candjcraft.com
Beads and other craft materials.

Clover USA
Tel: +1 800 233 1703
www.clover-usa.com
Sewing and general crafting supplies.

The Country Seat, Inc
Tel: +1 610 756 6124
www.countryseat.com
Online basket supplier, plus information and supplies to make your own.

Craft America
Tel: +1 800 407 5090
www.craftamerica.com
Selection of craft supplies.

Craft Site Directory
www.craftsitedirectory.com
Useful online resource.

CreateForLess
Tel: +1 866 333 4463
www.createforless.com
Craft and sewing supplies.

Hobby Lobby Stores, Inc.
Tel: +1 800 888 0321 ext. 1275
www.hobbylobby.com
Huge range of crafting materials.

Jo-Ann Fabric & Craft Stores
Tel: +1 888 739 4120
www.joann.com
Supplies fabric and crafting materials.

Land of Odds
Tel: +1 615 292 0610
www.landofodds.com
Beads and beading supplies.

Lazy K Crafts
www.lazykcrafts.com
Online suppliers of hand-woven decorative baskets.

Michaels Stores, Inc.
Tel: +1 800 642 4235
www.michaels.com
One of the largest US retailers of arts and crafts materials.

Purl
Tel: +1 212 420 8796
www.purlsoho.com
Materials, tools, notions, and accessories for sewing, knitting, and quilting.

Sugarcraft, Inc
www.sugarcraft.com
Icing flowers and other cake decorating supplies.

VCreative Designs
Tel: +1 705 322 8204
www.stencilsource.com
Stencils and stenciling accessories.

UK

Basket Basket
Tel: +44 (0)1420 476 791
www.basketbasket.co.uk
Great selection of baskets, including traditional French shopping baskets.

Calico Crafts
www.calicocrafts.co.uk
Online crafts specialist, supplying birch ply boxes ready for decorating, as well as vintage-style labels.

Cath Kidston
www.cathkidston.co.uk
Pretty vintage-style fabrics, as well as a selection of ribbons and ricrac braid.

Confetti
Tel: +44 (0)844 848 9797
www.confetti.co.uk
Selection of ribbons, feathers, and sequins, plus wrapping paper, blank cards, and envelopes.

Creations Art and Craft Materials
Tel: +44 (0)1326 555 777
www.ecreations.co.uk
Large stock of simple stitchcraft, stencils, paints, brushes, glues, and more.

Creative Beadcraft
Tel: +44 (0)1494 778 818
www.creativebeadcraft.co.uk
Huge selection of beads, as well as feathers, sequins, and tiny glass beads.

Hobbycraft
Tel: +44 (0)1202 596 100
www.hobbycraft.co.uk
Supplies ribbons, sequins, buttons, beads, pompoms, glue, papers, paints, stencil brushes and blank cards.

Homecrafts Direct
Tel: +44 (0)116 269 7733
www.homecrafts.co.uk
One of the UK's largest online arts and crafts suppliers.

Ikea
www.ikea.com
Good range of baskets, plus woven and wooden trays. Also seasonal selections of fun decorations, wrapping paper, and cards.

Jane Asher Party Cakes & Sugarcraft
Tel: +44 (0)20 7584 6177
www.jane-asher.co.uk
Icing in many colors, sugar flowers, presentation boxes, cookie cutters, plus plain or printed cellophane bags.

John Lewis
Tel: +44 (0)8456 049 049
www.johnlewis.com
Stocks a variety of baskets, fabrics, felt, wools, ribbons, threads, decorative beads and trims, as well as blank cards with envelopes.

Lakeland
Tel: +44 (0)1539 488 100
www.lakeland.co.uk
Crafting products including blank cards, ribbons, card kits, cellophane, decorative stamps and inks.

MacCulloch & Wallis
Tel: +44 (0)20 7629 0311
www.macculloch-wallis.co.uk
Stocks fabrics, interlinings and iron-on facings, as well as lace, ribbons, and other braids, buttons, appliqué motifs, and sewing threads.

More Than Gifts
Tel: +44 (0)115 974 6229
www.morethangifts.co.uk
Supplies blank Russian dolls ready to paint, as well as ready-painted dolls.

Paperchase
www.paperchase.co.uk
Handmade papers, crêpe and tissue paper, card, fabric-covered books, photograph albums, and blank cards.

S & J Woodcraft
Tel: +44 (0)1788 869 068
www.sandjwoodcraft.co.uk
Selection of MDF blanks to paint including coasters, tablemats, and letter racks. Will cut MDF letters to order.

Sew Essential
Tel: +44 (0)1922 722 276
www.sewessential.co.uk
Supplier of squared pattern paper as well as a variety of other sewing supplies.

Sewing and Craft Superstore
Tel: +44 (0)20 8767 0036
www.craftysewer.com
Everything from beads and sequins to blank cards, felt, pompoms, wool, buttons, and pipe cleaners.

The Stencil Library
Tel: +44 (0)1661 844 844
www.stencil-library.com
Decorative stencils, from simple shapes to complicated all-over designs, plus water-based stencil paints and brushes.

V V Rouleaux
Tel: +44 (0)20 7224 5179
www.vvrouleaux.com
Vast selection of ribbons from taffeta and velvet to embroidered cotton plus beaded motifs, pompoms, pretty trims, feather birds, and fabric flowers.

index

A
alphabet letters 17, 38, 106–107
appliqué 44, 94–97, 105, 123
apron, Father's Day 34–35, 116, 126

B
babies
  christening bunting 74
  layette basket 98–101, 124
  towel and facecloth 102–105,
    124, 125
bags
  evening 66–69, 120
  pompom 112–113
baskets
  baby layette 98–101, 124
  gardener's gift 60–63
  picnic 42–45, 120
  ring of roses 56–57
  spring bulb planter 64–65
beading
  candle votives 58–59
  chandelier drop heart 30, 32
  evening bag 66–69, 120
  flower corsage 28–29
  friendship bracelet 54–55
  photo album 46–49
  throw 88–91
blanket, appliqué 94–97, 123
bowl, papier mâché 12–13
bracelet, friendship 54–55
brooch, flower corsage 28–29
bunting, fabric 74–75, 125

C
candles 58–59, 76–77
card, new home 72–73, 119
cellphone case 114–115, 121
chair, stenciled 108–109
Christmas
  candied orange peel 24–25
  clove pomander 22–23
  stocking 18–21, 117, 126
coasters 82, 84–85
cookies 10–11
corsage, flower 28–29
cushions see pillows

D
decoupage 36–37, 84–85, 109
doilies 74, 82
dolls, Russian 110–111

E
Easter
  bowl 12–13, 17
  cookies 10

egg cozies 14–15, 119
  painted eggs 16–17
engagement pillow 38, 118–119

F
Father's Day, apron 34–35, 116, 126
flowers
  appliqué 81, 97, 123
  corsage 28–29
  Easter bowl 12–13
  embroidered pillow 86–87
  felt 38
  spring bulb planter 64–65

G
gardeners
  gift basket 60–63
  spring bulb planter 64–65
gift tags 7, 101, 124

H
hearts
  chandelier drop 30–33, 116
  gift tag 101
  lavender 30, 52–53, 116, 121
  monogrammed pillows 38–41,
    118–119
  Valentine cookies 10

I
lavender hearts 30, 52–53, 116, 121

M
Mother's Day, flower corsage 28–29

N
new home card 72–73, 119

O
oranges
  candied orange peel 24–25
  clove pomander 22–23

P
painting
  alphabet letters 106–107
  eggs 16–17
  Russian dolls 110
papier mâché, Easter bowl 12–13, 17
photo album, beaded 46–49
picnic basket and rug 42–45, 120
picture frame, decoupage 36–37
pillows
  appliqué 81, 94
  embroidered 86–87
  monogrammed hearts 38–41,
    118–119

pomander, clove 22–23
pompoms 112–113
pots, stenciled 62–63

S
sewing/embroidery projects
  appliqué blanket 94–97, 123
  baby basket 98–101
  baby towel/facecloth 102–105,
    124–125
  beaded throw/wrap 88–91
  chandelier drop heart 30–33, 116
  Christmas stockings 18–21, 117,
    126
  evening bag 66–69, 120
  fabric bunting 74–75, 125
  Father's Day apron 34–35, 116,
126
  felt cellphone case 114–115, 121
  felt egg cozies 14–15, 119
  lavender hearts 30, 52–53, 121
  patchwork teapot cozy 78–81, 122
  picnic basket and rug 42–45, 120
  pillows 38–41, 81, 86–87, 118–119
stenciling
  apron 34–35, 116, 126
  child's chair 108–109
  gardener's gift basket 60–61
  wooden tray 82–83

T
table decorations 58–59, 76–77, 82,
  84
teapot cozy, patchwork 78–81, 122
throw, beaded 88–91
toiletries basket 56–57
towels 44, 102–103, 125
tray, stenciled 82–83
trug, stenciled 60–61

V
Valentine's Day cookies 10–11

W
weddings
  beaded photo album 46–49
  bridesmaid's bag 69
  bunting 74
  monogrammed pillows 38, 118–119
wrap, beaded evening 91

Author's acknowledgments

Thanks to the Stencil Library and to
Hobbycraft for providing wonderful
stencils and craft materials for the book.

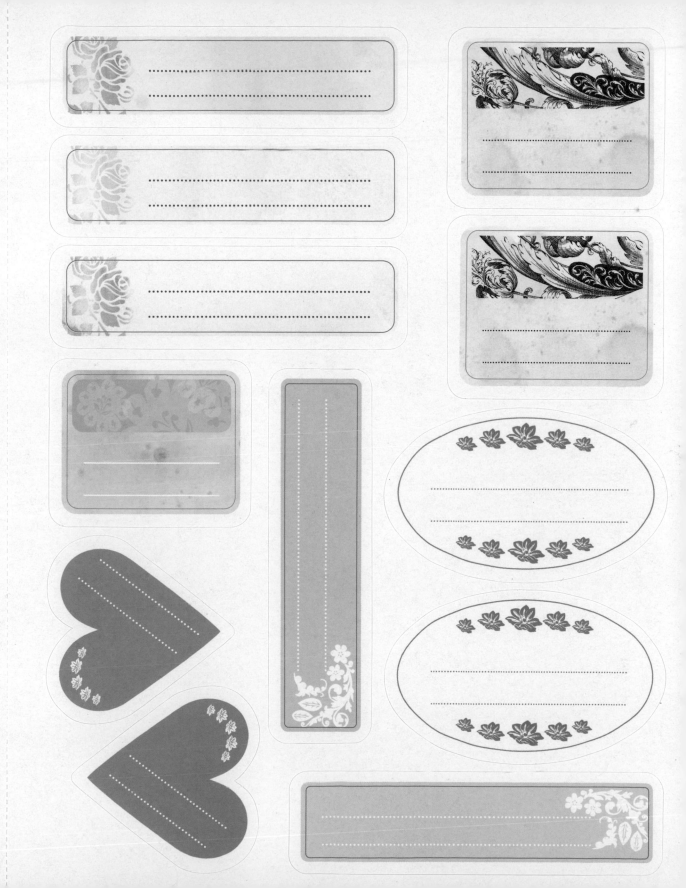